WELCOME TO THE HEART OF NE(

The Neolithic remains on Orkney make it a very special place indeed. Nowhere else in northern Europe can you visit 5,000-year-old villages alongside the spectacular ritual and burial monuments created by their inhabitants. The modern farming landscape abounds with these exceptionally well-preserved ancient monuments, and much more besides.

The Heart of Neolithic Orkney became a World Heritage Site in 1999, a mark of its international significance. It lies in the west of Mainland, Orkney's largest island, around 25 miles (40km) from the north-eastern tip of mainland Scotland.

The Heart of Neolithic Orkney is a modern idea, but the area was clearly an important place in the past. Its other distinctive qualities – the setting of sea, lochs and the natural amphitheatre of hills, the wildlife and the sound, light and smells – all amplify the experience of today's visitors just as they did 5,000 years ago.

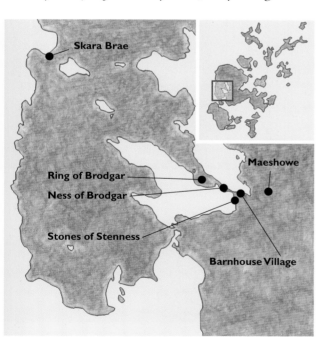

Opposite: The Ring of Brodgar.

Above: A map of the Orkney mainland, showing key sites in and around the World Heritage Site.

HIGHLIGHTS

The Neolithic and Early Bronze Age buildings and monuments that form the World Heritage Site date from between 5,100 and 3,500 years ago.

These monuments are all in State care and comprise some of the best preserved and best known sites, but they are not alone. They sit within a wider, multi-period archaeological landscape. There are many well-preserved Neolithic and later monuments throughout Orkney.

▼ BARNHOUSE VILLAGE
This settlement shows us that in Neolithic times Skara Brae was far from unique (p.24).

▲ NORSE GRAFFITI
Many centuries after Maeshowe fell out of use, Norse men and women left their mark on the walls of the tomb. This is now the largest collection of runes outside Scandinavia (pp.18–23).

▲ MAESHOWE
This burial mound is arguably the finest Neolithic building in north-west Europe, ingeniously aligned so that its interior is illuminated by the setting sun at midwinter (p.8).

◄ SKARA BRAE

The most complete Neolithic village in north-west Europe, Skara Brae allows us to see prehistoric houses up close (p.44).

▼ THE RING OF BRODGAR

This massive stone circle and henge remained the focus for ritual activity after the Neolithic period (p.36).

▼ THE WATCHSTONE

Now standing alone near the Stones of Stenness, this was one of a pair guarding access to the strip of sacred ground between the two lochs (pp.30–1).

▲ THE STONES OF STENNESS

Earlier and less expansive than the Ring of Brodgar, this ceremonial henge site is dominated by huge standing stones, unusually set around a central hearth (pp.28–9).

▲ ARCHAEOLOGICAL RESEARCH

We are hungry for more knowledge. New discoveries such as the Ness of Brodgar continue to surprise us (p.62).

INTRODUCTION:
THE NEOLITHIC LANDSCAPE

The Heart of Neolithic Orkney occupies a particular kind of place. Maeshowe and its neighbouring monuments were built on low-lying land around the Lochs of Harray and Stenness, surrounded by a natural amphitheatre of hills.

This bowl-shaped setting is likely to have been significant. Elsewhere in northern Britain, other late Neolithic monuments are often found in similar locations. Machrie Moor on the Isle of Arran is another example.

Today, an isthmus, or strip of land, runs between the two lochs. In Neolithic times, the water level of the lochs was lower, making the isthmus wider, but it was still a narrow land bridge between two bodies of water.

The Loch of Stenness gives direct access to the open sea, while the Loch of Harray is today mainly freshwater. But it was not always like that. When the first farmers arrived in Orkney, lower sea-levels meant that both lochs were still fresh.

The Neolithic farmers who worked the land around the lochs were living in a changing landscape. We can only wonder how prehistoric peoples regarded this changing crossroads of land and sea, freshwater and brine.

When work started at Maeshowe, in the later Neolithic, most of the original woodland that grew in Orkney had gone, leaving the open landscape that we know today. The islands were populated by farms and villages, interspersed with burial and ceremonial places.

The surrounding land would have been a mixture of small plots used for growing crops, pastoral grassland for grazing sheep and cattle, scrub, woodland and heather moorland.

Above: Maeshowe (centre right) with the Lochs of Harray and Stenness beyond.

Top right: A 'Skaill knife' with Neolithic decoration. Many tools of this kind were found at Skara Brae, with a sharp edge created by splitting a flat stone.

THE BIGGER PICTURE

The sites that form the Heart of Neolithic Orkney are only the tip of the iceberg. An extensive archaeological landscape survives beneath and between these monuments, much of it invisible to the eye, though it has been detected through geophysical surveys.

When visiting these sites it is important to consider the landscape as more than a cluster of surviving monuments. Instead, try to imagine it as a tapestry into which the lives of humans, monuments and artefacts are interwoven. Think of a very old fabric, reworked through time, with losses, additions and repairs. The many people who have worked on it each brought their own memories and motivations to the landscape.

Human settlement involves a constant reworking of the environment, but some activities have a bigger impact than others.

Some of Orkney's Neolithic sites have been more vulnerable to change, particularly from coastal erosion or agricultural activity. Barnhouse Village provided a ready supply of building stone for local use. The ceremonial sites, with their big banks, ditches and standing stones, have often survived better, perhaps because later generations continued to respect them.

As farming intensified in the 19th and 20th centuries, it reduced the number of monuments and changed the nature of the land in Orkney. Over the same period, antiquarians and archaeologists also altered the appearance and form of monuments through excavations and reconstruction.

UNPICKING THE PAST

The impact of all these activities is cumulative. Our challenge is to unpick the landscape and to understand society through time, while caring for the evidence that survives.

We shall never know the full truth about what happened here, but we constantly edge towards better and subtler understandings. Our ability to do this depends on the nature, quality and extent of our investigations and how we interpret them.

Our methods for recording, investigating and dating these monuments continue to improve and new evidence is continually coming to light. As our understanding develops, we can move a little closer to answering the question that all these monuments demand of us: how did people experience their real and imagined worlds 5,000 years ago?

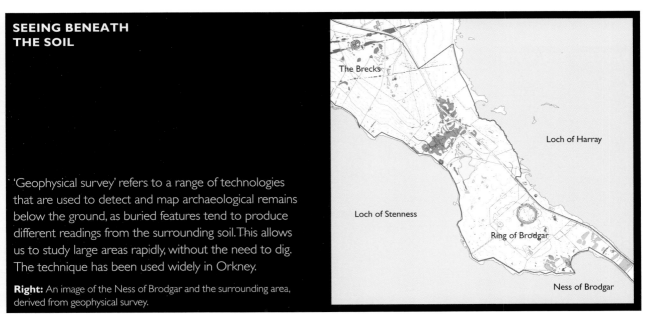

SEEING BENEATH THE SOIL

'Geophysical survey' refers to a range of technologies that are used to detect and map archaeological remains below the ground, as buried features tend to produce different readings from the surrounding soil. This allows us to study large areas rapidly, without the need to dig. The technique has been used widely in Orkney.

Right: An image of the Ness of Brodgar and the surrounding area, derived from geophysical survey.

The Brecks

Loch of Harray

Loch of Stenness

Ring of Brodgar

Ness of Brodgar

EXPLORE NEOLITHIC ORKNEY

Modern paths and roads determine how we approach and experience the sites in the Neolithic landscape today. But our ancestors may have approached them in quite different ways.

You can visit these monuments in any order you choose, although there is a logic to visiting Barnhouse before Stones of Stenness. Walking is a good way to appreciate how the monuments are situated in the landscape.

1 Ring of Bookan

2 Bookan cairns

3 Bookan chambered cairn

4 Wasbister house

5 Wasbister disc barrow

6 Dyke o' Sean

7 Ring of Brodgar

8 Salt Knowe

9 Plumcake Mound

10 Fresh Knowe

11 Comet Stone

12 South Knowe

13 Ness of Brodgar

14 Watchstone

15 Barnhouse Village

16 Stones of Stenness

17 Barnhouse Stone

18 Maeshowe

19 Unstan chambered cairn

P Parking

-- RSPB Reserve

... Footpath

VISITING THE SITES

The World Heritage Site includes Maeshowe, Skara Brae, the Stones of Stenness and the Ring of Brodgar.

Admission charges apply for Maeshowe (for which you need to pre-book) and Skara Brae.

The Stones of Stenness and Ring of Brodgar are free and open at all times, and our Ranger Service offers free guided walks, also covering the Ness of Brodgar when it is open.

For more information call the Ranger Service: **01856 841 732**, or our staff at Skara Brae: **01856 841 815**.

The sites listed in red above are on private land, so please remember to follow the Scottish Outdoor Access Code.

www.outdooraccess-scotland.com

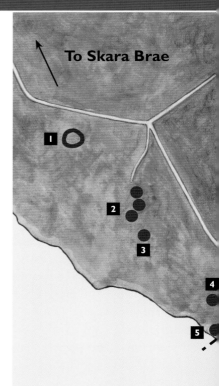

To Skara Brae

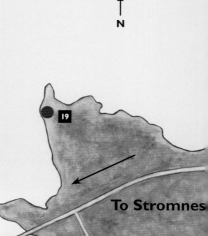

N

To Stromness

Loch of Harray

6 P

9

7

10

11

12

Loch of Stenness

13

15

14

P 16

18

17

Stenness

To Kirkwall

MAESHOWE

Maeshowe is the finest chambered tomb in north-west Europe. Its large, grassy mound is a prominent feature of the local landscape.

The mound sits on a circular platform surrounded by a ditch and, beyond this, a bank. Within the mound, a long entrance passage leads into a grand stone-lined chamber with side-cells. Tombs like Maeshowe are sometimes called passage graves.

'Howe' derives from the Old Norse for a hill, but the origin of 'Maes' is not clear.

While the mound may appear to be separate from the complex of monuments on the Brodgar isthmus, Maeshowe was deliberately located to form a significant part of this Neolithic ceremonial landscape.

It is clearly visible from the isthmus between the lochs, and many of the other monuments in this area align with or have views to Maeshowe.

Below: An illustration of Maeshowe dating from around 1862.

One challenge when visiting Maeshowe is to link what you discover inside the tomb to what lies outside it. You are sure to be awed by its atmosphere, as well as the Neolithic building skills and the Norse runes, but spare some time for the rest of the monument and its relationship to the landscape.

BUILT TO IMPRESS

Maeshowe was built around 5,000 years ago, and its builders clearly intended to make an impact. Many other tombs in Orkney have a similar form, but Maeshowe is by far the most elaborate and sophisticated.

Many hands carried stones and clay to build the mound, and many more excavated the ditch – all without the aid of metal tools or powered machinery. There is no doubt that its construction was a major enterprise and a tremendous social commitment.

Opposite: A view of Maeshowe from the west.

BUILDING MAESHOWE

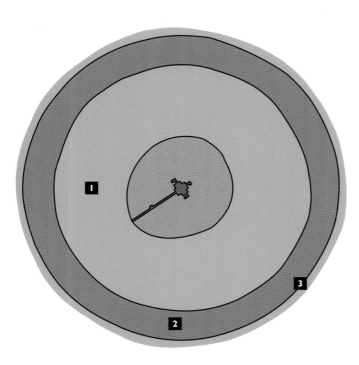

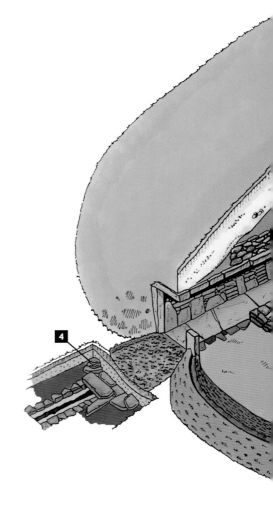

Despite its outward appearance as an almost natural grassy mound, the construction of Maeshowe is deceptively complex.

We have learned a great deal about the site's development and sophisticated design from archaeological investigation in the 1950s, 1970s and 1990s.

The 1990s excavations revealed tantalising suggestions that this site has a much longer history. It may already have been significant to the local community long before the tomb was built. Some archaeologists suggest that the platform and surrounding ditch were constructed before the tomb, perhaps forming an earlier ceremonial monument.

▮ PLATFORM

The mound sits on a large, roughly circular platform, formed by ingenious sculpting of a natural glacial mound. This was levelled using clay from local sources.

Above left: A plan showing the mound within the wider structure of the platform and ditch.

Above right: A cutaway illustration of Maeshowe mound, showing its internal structure.

▮ DITCH

About three-quarters of the platform's circumference is encircled by a wide ditch, dug out from the bedrock. It has a flat bottom and would have been about 2m deep. This kind of ditch around a passage grave is exceptionally rare. It is not clear how it would have been crossed. At least one sizeable standing stone stood at the edge of the ditch, but it is not clear whether the stone stood at the same time as the mound.

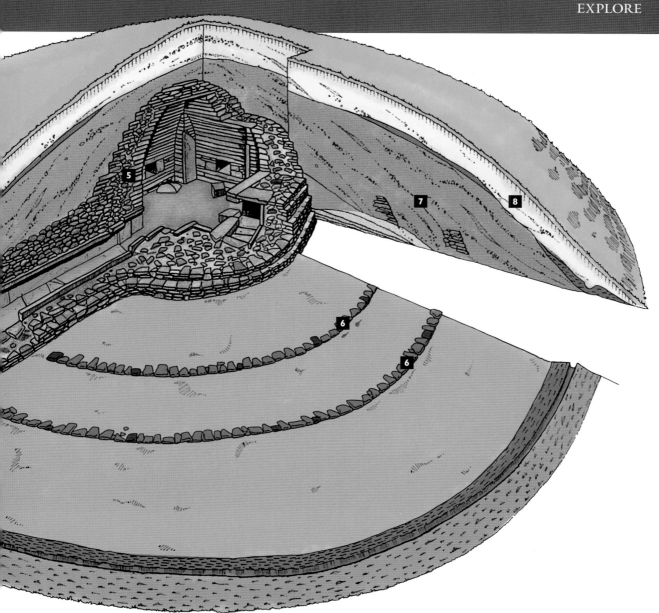

3 WALL & BANK

Beyond the ditch there is evidence that an outer stone wall originally ran around the site. Its original height is unknown, but it could have been substantial. This wall is now concealed under a more recent turf bank.

4 DRAIN

Archaeologists digging in front of the entrance to the tomb discovered a stone 'drain' that seems to relate to an earlier building, possibly a house.

5 INNER STRUCTURE

The central chamber is encased by a well-built wall that steps inward up to the roof.

6 OUTER WALLS

The inner walls are surrounded by two low walls that retain the stone packing.

7 CLAY LAYER

The whole structure is covered by a substantial layer of clay and small stones. The builders used yellow clay, which they probably carried in baskets from the Loch of Harray.

8 OUTER SKIN

The whole structure was sealed by a clay skin, using the same yellow clay. This is now hidden under a turf covering.

The resulting mound is about 35m across and 7m high. It is a carefully crafted, robust and watertight structure to which access could be carefully controlled.

The soft, rounded exterior of today masks a starkly different interior space, where darkness and the straight lines of stones predominate.

INSIDE THE TOMB

The interior of Maeshowe feels quite remote from the outside world, and this helps alert our senses to the qualities of the space.

Entering the dark interior via the long narrow passage feels like stepping into another world, or into the earth itself – and feelings like these may well have been important in the past. The grand scale and impressive architecture of Maeshowe can only be fully appreciated once inside.

For most of their length, the walls of the entrance passage are formed from single massive stone slabs. The largest of these weighs around three tonnes. They have been compared to the largest uprights at the Stones of Stenness and may indeed have been standing stones at some point. This is an extraordinary achievement of engineering in an age before machinery – or even metal tools.

THE MAIN CHAMBER AND STONE UPRIGHTS

In contrast to the massive mound around it, the main chamber measures only 4.7m across by 4.5m high, yet as we enter from the cramped passage its height is impressive. The drystone walls of the chamber are built from massive stone slabs, meticulously aligned to create flush vertical walls.

The roof of the main chamber is a vault formed by slightly overlapping stone slabs, most of which span the complete width of each wall. The chamber may originally have been higher, but the top was removed when curious Norse visitors – and, much later, Victorians – broke into the mound.

In the early 1860s, Mr Balfour, who then owned Maeshowe, built a distinctly modern roof over the chamber. Today that roof is capped by a concrete slab, hidden in the mound above. The modern elements have been painted white to distinguish them from the Neolithic stonework.

Above: The interior of the tomb, looking west toward the entrance passage.

Opposite: An image derived from 3D scanning, showing the long entrance passage, the central chamber and the three side chambers.

At each corner of the main chamber is a magnificent upright, a standing stone encased within a pier – or corner block – of smaller stones. These four uprights almost certainly formed the earliest part of Maeshowe's construction. They dictated the height of the roof, though they do not have a structural function. One theory is that they helped to define the correct alignment of the chamber and passage so that they would catch the midwinter sunset.

Another theory suggests that the corner stones originally stood elsewhere, as standing stones. Whatever their role, their prominence in the tomb suggests they held some significance to the community who built Maeshowe.

THE SIDE CELLS AND ROOF

A side cell, or chamber, is built into the middle of each of the three walls around the entrance. Two of these cells contain a low platform (the third may have done so originally). In contrast to similar tombs, the floor, back wall and ceiling of the side chambers are formed of single large slabs.

Large stones lie on the floor below the opening to each of the side cells. These may have once been used to seal the chambers. There is also a blocking stone contained within a recess towards the outer end of the entrance passage. This stone balances on a pivot and could be swung inwards to seal the tomb from the inside.

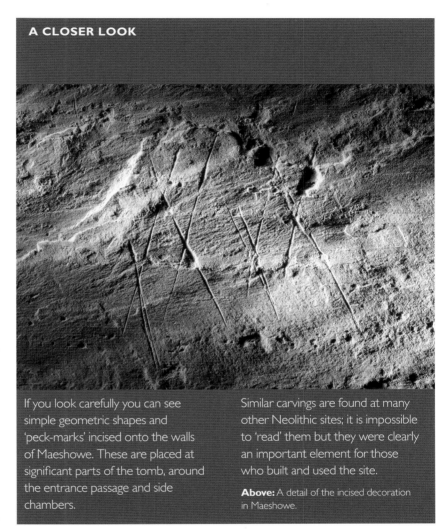

A CLOSER LOOK

If you look carefully you can see simple geometric shapes and 'peck-marks' incised onto the walls of Maeshowe. These are placed at significant parts of the tomb, around the entrance passage and side chambers.

Similar carvings are found at many other Neolithic sites; it is impossible to 'read' them but they were clearly an important element for those who built and used the site.

Above: A detail of the incised decoration in Maeshowe.

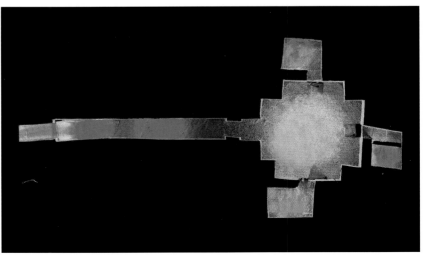

MIDWINTER AT MAESHOWE

Maeshowe was designed to mark midwinter, an important point in the year for Neolithic society.

For three weeks before and after the shortest day of the year (21 December), the light of the setting sun shines straight down the gently sloping passageway into the tomb and illuminates the back of the chamber. As the sun sinks behind the hills of Hoy, its rays first hit the Barnhouse Stone, standing to the south-west, before reaching Maeshowe itself.

Midwinter must have been significant for all early farming communities, marking the shortest day of the year and the changing of the seasons. It seems that the cycles of life and death were linked to the annual cycle of the seasons; the death of one year and the rebirth of another. Alignment with aspects of the winter or summer solstices is a feature of some other Neolithic passage graves too.

One example is Newgrange, in Ireland's Boyne Valley. In contrast to Maeshowe, the midwinter sun lights Newgrange's chamber at sunrise rather than sunset. For one day only, the sun's rays are channelled through a carefully designed opening above the entrance passage, shining light through the cairn and into the chamber.

At Maeshowe, celebrants may have pivoted the massive blocking stone in the passageway to create a similar effect. This would have heightened the midwinter experience for those inside by focusing a narrow beam of light on to the back of the chamber, which would slowly move as the sun sets.

Top: An illustration of 1875 shows light pouring through the entrance passage to illuminate the interior.

Middle: The Barnhouse Stone, which was carefully aligned to catch the rays of the setting midwinter sun just before they reached Maeshowe's entrance passage.

Bottom: Newgrange Neolithic tomb in Ireland, aligned so that light enters the chamber at sunrise in midwinter.

Opposite: The chamber at the back (north-east) of Maeshowe, lit as it would be at sunset in midwinter.

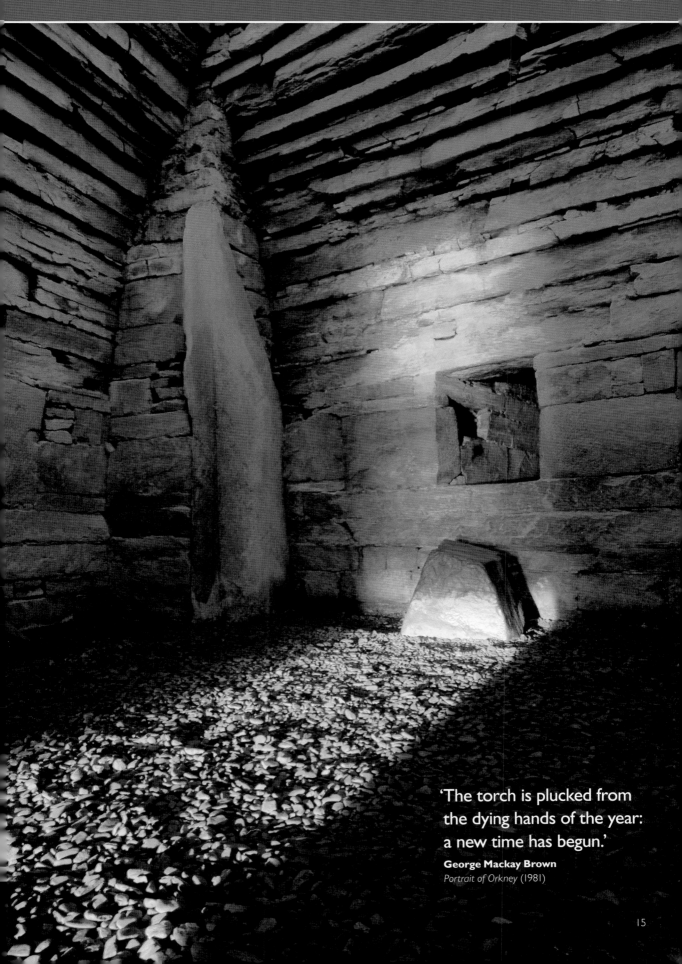

'The torch is plucked from
the dying hands of the year:
a new time has begun.'

George Mackay Brown
Portrait of Orkney (1981)

BURIALS
AT MAESHOWE

Archaeologists believe that Maeshowe may have been used for the burial of significant members of the community, but this conclusion is far from straightforward.

The tomb has been disturbed many times in the past, and its clearance in the 1800s was not scientifically carried out. As a result, the only recorded finds are a few fragments of human skull and some horse bones, which have now been lost.

Bones do not always survive the passage of time, but excavation at some similar monuments has revealed human bones, within the chambers.

The chambered cairn at Quanterness, 6 miles (10km) east of Maeshowe, is one such site. Here, archaeologists found the remains of more than 157 individuals of all ages, and estimate that it could have originally held the remains of around 400 people.

The evidence for human remains found in Orkney's Neolithic tombs varies considerably. In some cases whole skeletons have been found, but it is more common to find disarticulated individual bones within the chambers.

Sometimes these individual bones appear to have been sorted or carefully organised and placed in different parts of the tomb. Evidence suggests that individual bones were periodically rearranged or cleared throughout a tomb's long period of use.

New techniques of analysis help us to learn more about the dead. Isotope analysis can reveal details of the Neolithic diet and where a person grew up. Other studies are examining information relating to illness and even the levels of violence within the community.

Research suggests that not everyone who died was laid to rest in a tomb like Maeshowe, though we have yet to establish the criteria for inclusion. Perhaps only significant ancestors could be buried here.

CEREMONIES OF THE DEAD
Neolithic tombs such as Maeshowe were not only built as final resting places for the dead. They were designed for repeated access by the living, and the excavated evidence suggests that activity inside the tomb may have included ceremonies on behalf of the wider community. As Maeshowe is the largest and most sophisticated tomb we can speculate that it may have been important for all who lived in Neolithic Orkney.

THE NORSE DISCOVERY

After many centuries of abandonment, Maeshowe was rediscovered in the 1100s by a group of Norse travellers. They recorded their visit with a wealth of remarkable graffiti.

After it was built, Maeshowe was used for several hundred years, then sealed and abandoned, perhaps because of changing beliefs and practices. At least 3,000 years passed before it attracted any significant human interest that archaeologists have been able to detect.

Then, in the middle of the 1100s AD, the Norse – descendants of the Vikings – broke into the mound. As a testament of their discovery, they left light-hearted carvings all over the walls of the tomb, in the form of at least 33 runic inscriptions and eight sketches.

This graffiti comprises the largest collection of runic inscriptions that survives outside Scandinavia – a potent reminder that Orkney was under Norwegian rule until 1468.

From the late 700s, pagan Vikings from Norway began raiding in Scotland. Some raiders settled in Orkney, establishing a semi-independent Norse earldom and a staging post on the major trading route between Ireland and Scandinavia. By the 1100s, these Norse settlers had adopted Christian beliefs, and Orkney was a place of considerable cultural achievements. Kirkwall grew into a flourishing urban centre and in 1137 work began on its splendid Romanesque cathedral, dedicated to St Magnus. Orkney's Norse earls were wealthy and well-travelled, with extensive connections.

The *Orkneyinga Saga*, written in the early 1200s, tells their story. It is here that Maeshowe is first mentioned in surviving written sources, and here too that we learn of at least one occasion when the Norse visited it.

ORKAHAUGR

The Norse knew Maeshowe by a different name. Shortly after Christmas 1153, Earl Harald Maddadarson was travelling over land from Hamnavoe (Stromness) to Firth (the Finstown area). Caught in a snowstorm, he and his men took shelter in 'Orkahaugr', and the location of Maeshowe fits the story as described in the *Orkneyinga Saga*.

Maeshowe is also the only *haugr* (howe) that we know the Norse broke into. The implication is that the tomb was already accessible and the properties of its interior familiar.

References in the runes to 'Jerusalem-travellers', or pilgrims, tell us that the Norse entered Maeshowe on at least one earlier occasion. One carving, by the (female) cook, Líf, seems to refer to Earl Rognvald.

The *Orkneyinga Saga* records how Earl Rognvald gathered his men together in 1150–51 to travel first to Rome and onwards to Jerusalem, in a great pilgrimage. The pilgrims gave themselves the credit for breaking into the tomb, and this would fit with the later entry of Harald and his men in 1153.

Above: Two of the carved corbels in St Magnus Cathedral, Kirkwall, depicting human faces. The cathedral was built by the Norse aristocracy in the mid-1100s, around the time when Earl Harald broke into Maeshowe.

SOUTH-EAST WALL
Guide to the runic graffiti

1 'This mound was built before Lothbrok's.
Her sons, they were bold; such were men, as
they were of themselves [i.e. they were the sort
of people you could really call men]. Jerusalem-
travellers broke Orkhaugr. Líf, the Earl's
housekeeper, carved. In the north–west great
treasure is hidden. It was long ago that great
treasure was hidden here. Happy is he who can
find the great wealth. Hakon alone carried
treasure out of this mound. Simon. Sigrith.'
In this group of individual carvings men and women
banter with each other in a light-hearted manner.

2 'The man who is most skilled in runes west
of the ocean carved these runes with the axe
which Gauk Trandilsson owned in the south
of the country [Iceland].'
Two different types of runes are used here.

3 'Ingigerth is the most beautiful ...'
The sketch of a slavering dog next to this inscription
suggests an appreciation of Ingigerth's feminine qualities.

4 'Ofram Sigurdsson carved these runes.'
This inscription came away from the wall shortly after
its 19th-century discovery.

5 'Hermund hard … carved runes.'

6 'Arnfinn Food carved these runes.'
Several of the inscriptions appear to include nicknames,
so perhaps Arnfinn was a greedy man.

7 'Benedikt made this cross.'
We do not know which of the crosses within
the tomb this refers to.

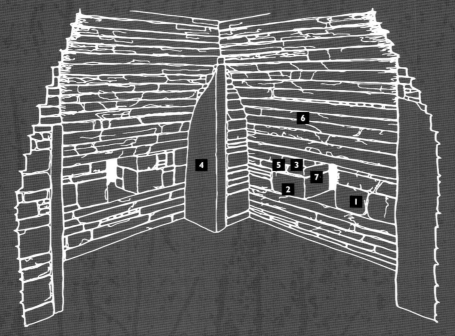

SOUTH-WEST AND NORTH-WEST WALLS
Guide to the runic graffiti

1 ᚠᚢᚦᚨᚱᚲᚺᚾᛁᛁᛒᛣᚲᛏᛇᛙᛂᛁᚠᛟ

'fuþorkhniastbmtyæǫøeg-.'
A version of the runic alphabet used at Maeshowe.

2 'Ingibiorg the fair widow. Many a woman has gone stooping in here. A great show–off. Erling.' Does this mean that all or part of the passage to the tomb was open at this time? The Norse selected flat surfaces to work on, usually avoiding the areas of Neolithic pick-marking. Here, however, you can see a band of pecking underneath the inscription.

3 'That will be true which I say, that treasure was carried away. Treasure was carried away three nights before they broke this mound.'

4 ' … is told to me that treasure is hidden here well enough. Few say as Odd Orkason said in those runes which he cut.'

5 'Thorni bedded. Helgi carved.'

6 'Eyjolf Kolbeinsson carved these runes high.' A lot of effort went into achieving this boast!

7 'That is a Viking … then came underneath to this place.'

8 'Otarr … carved these runes.'

9 'Vemund carved.'

10 'Thorir … '

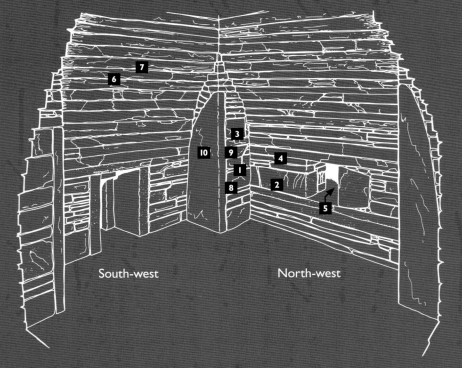

South-west   North-west

UNDERSTANDING THE RUNES

The angular letters used in Maeshowe belong to runic alphabets developed by Germanic peoples from the 2nd century AD.

Derived in part from the Roman alphabet, these letters could easily be carved onto stone, wood or bone. We find them used for inscriptions, graffiti, everyday messages and magical formulae.

The standard runic alphabet, as used by Norse people in the 1100s, is known as fuþork (þ, thorn, is pronounced 'th'). It had 16 letters: fuþork – hnias – tbmly.

On the south-west wall of Maeshowe, one person carved the whole fuþork alphabet, although they muddled the last three letters. In fact, a fuller range of letters is used at Maeshowe.

TWIG RUNES

If the Norse wanted to be clever, or to tease their readers, they wrote in a cryptic alphabet known as twig runes. At Maeshowe, someone called Erling signed his name in twig runes on the north-west wall.

On the south-east wall a man styling himself 'most skilled in runes west of the ocean' showed off by beginning in twig runes and progressing to standard runes.

INTERPRETING THE RUNES

It is one thing to know the runic characters, but quite another thing to work out which letters are represented on the walls of the tomb, and to make sense of what they say in Old Norse. Sometimes this is straightforward, but we are left with gaps and uncertainties, particularly when the inscriptions are worn. Often the translations are tentative at best.

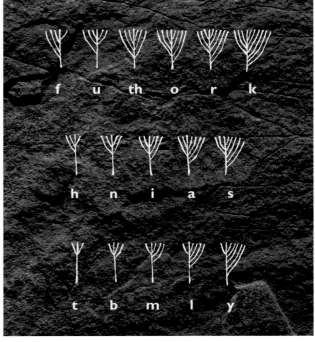

Top: How to read the 'fuþork' runes used at Maeshowe.

Right: How to read the 'twig' runes.

TALES OF TREASURE

Norse inscriptions on three sides of the tomb refer to treasure. What do these references mean?

We do not know what the Norse found when they broke into the tomb. The side chambers may have contained human bones and pottery or stone tools, but we can be confident that nothing left by the Neolithic people would have been considered treasure by the Norse.

It has been suggested that pagan Vikings may have re-used the tomb for a high-status burial in the 800s or 900s. Fine metalwork could accompany such burials, and would certainly have constituted 'treasure' for any Norse who came across it several centuries later. We cannot rule this possibility out, but there is no evidence to support it.

Instead, we need to imagine what the Norse who rediscovered the tomb would have felt – the impact of this dark and wondrous cavern perhaps inspired these claims of treasure. Storytelling was an important part of Norse life, and 'Orkahaugr' clearly developed its own mythology as an important place in Orcadian folklore, as its mention in the *Orkneyinga Saga* suggests.

DRAGON OR LION?

This curious carving is often referred to as the Maeshowe 'dragon', though some interpret it as a lion. It is a famous image that combines Romanesque and late Viking artistic features. Art historians have dated it to around AD 1150, but it is reminiscent of earlier animal figures found on carved stones and metalwork across Scandinavia.

Above right: One of the Lewis Chessmen. These playing pieces were made from walrus ivory by Norse craftsmen in the mid-1100s, around the time of Earl Harald's visit to Maeshowe.

NORTH-EAST WALL
Guide to the runic graffiti

1. The 'Maeshowe lion', or dragon.

2. 'Jerusalem men broke this mound.'

3. 'Arnfinn, son of Steinn, carved these runes.'

4. ' … carved these runes.'
   The form of runes used here is unparalleled anywhere else.

5. 'Orm the … carved.'
   Orm was perhaps 'the younger'.

6. 'Ogmund carved … '

7. This was probably a name, but is difficult to interpret.

8. A number of vertical lines – possibly the initial stage in the carving of a runic inscription.

9. A knotted serpent or snake.

10. An animal – possibly a walrus, otter or seal – as well as some individual runic letters.

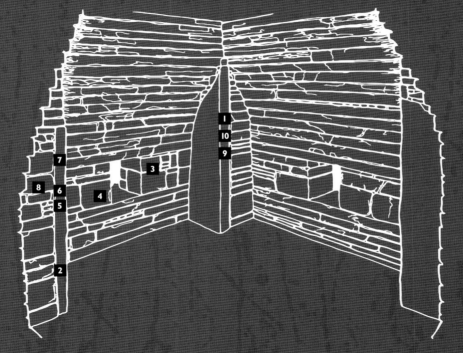

BARNHOUSE VILLAGE

In 1984 the archaeologist Colin Richards discovered and excavated a settlement in the field alongside the Stones of Stenness. The discovery of the foundations of a late Neolithic village here transformed our understanding of this landscape, making it one of the most important archaeological finds in Britain in the late 20th century.

Understanding Barnhouse helps us to interpret what we see at the other sites in Orkney. The presence of a residential settlement at the heart of what had previously been considered a ceremonial landscape showed that, rather than being set apart from daily life, these monuments were an integral element of it.

The people who lived at Barnhouse from around 3200 BC to 2900 BC must have frequented the Stones of Stenness (which they may have raised) and Maeshowe – both monuments are visible from Barnhouse. They could also have known people who lived at Skara Brae – indeed some of the houses at Barnhouse (and the objects found in them) are similar to the early houses at Skara Brae.

DEVELOPMENT OF THE VILLAGE

The earliest houses at Barnhouse date to around 3200 BC. Once established, the community grew quickly. Archaeologists have excavated the remains of up to 14 buildings. Excavation indicated that people had constructed a series of houses on the same site, and most of the houses experienced many phases of rebuilding.

At the heart of the village was an open area, where evidence suggests people prepared animal skins, made pottery and crafted stone tools. Outside the houses there was evidence of the disposal of rubbish, including decayed roofing materials.

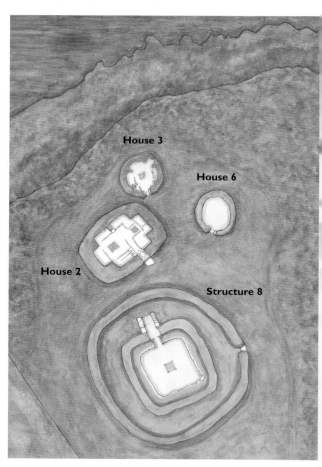

Above: A map showing the structures now visible at Barnhouse Village.

Opposite above: Structure 8.

Opposite below: Barnhouse Village as it may have looked at a later stage in its development, with Structure 8 under construction.

UNDERSTANDING THE BUILDINGS

Barnhouse today is a modern reconstruction of the foundations of just four buildings.

This represents only a part of the settlement, and these four buildings were originally constructed and used at different dates. The timber uprights indicate where archaeologists found sockets for wooden posts that might relate to internal divisions or furniture.

Like Skara Brae, the dwellings uncovered at Barnhouse have central hearths, stone furniture and recessed spaces. However, House 2 and Structure 8 have features that suggest they were more than simply houses.

These two buildings have complex layouts, which would have restricted visibility and movement around the interior. This hints at social organisation and varying social roles in the community at Barnhouse.

HOUSE 6

The layout of House 6 and the items found here suggest that it had a specialist function. Originally, it seems to have been laid out like a typical house, but by the end of its long occupation this had changed. Many worked flints and pumice were found here, suggesting that it may have been used for the specialised working of bone, wood or animal skins.

HOUSE 3

One of the earliest dwellings at Barnhouse, House 3 shares features with the houses at Skara Brae. Its entrance leads into a square space with a central hearth. To the right and left are large stone boxes, while on the back wall is a 'dresser'. These features are usually interpreted as beds and shelving, but we cannot be sure.

HOUSE 2

Built on a clay platform, House 2 is larger and more prominently sited than the others. It was one of the earliest structures built at Barnhouse. Its walls are of high-quality masonry – the builders clearly intended it to be seen and its exterior stonework to stand apart

It maintained its original form throughout the occupation of the site, suggesting an enduring significance to the community.

The interior is complex – and comparable to the tombs at Quoyness and Quanterness in a number of ways. It contains not one but two large stone hearths, and originally had settings of stone and wood that restricted access around the house.

Leading from the entrance, there is a central passage which opens into the eastern (right hand) area, in which the stone furniture dictated movement in an anti-clockwise direction.

To enter the western half of the house, people would have had to cross a cist (stone box) containing bones. Excavation suggested that cooking and eating may have taken place in the eastern half, while the more secluded western half was set aside for the manufacture of stone maceheads – high-status objects.

STRUCTURE 8

Structure 8 was constructed towards the end of the village's life, when many of the dwellings had been abandoned, and seems to mark a big change in use of the site.

Its form and scale suggest it was not a house at all. It stands near the edge of the earlier village, on the site of a large, open hearth, around which cooking and eating had taken place.

Like Maeshowe, Structure 8 is founded on a clay platform and a substantial stone wall surrounds it. The internal floor space is almost double that at Maeshowe. It included fittings such as a wide stone bench around the walls, a possible dresser and a large central hearth.

At the entrance is an unusual porch arrangement that incorporates a fireplace. This may have had a symbolic role, to do with purification or transformation, though it may not have been visible once the building was completed.

Curiously, the hearth was identical in shape and size to a hearth at the centre of the Stones of Stenness. Archaeologists have suggested that the hearth slabs may have been taken there from Barnhouse.

Right: A cutaway illustration showing how the interior of House 2 may have looked.

THE STONES OF STENNESS

This is the oldest ceremonial monument in the World Heritage Site, located close to Barnhouse. As we approach from the village, we follow in the footsteps of the people who built and used the site.

Dating for the construction of the Stones of Stenness is frustratingly uncertain – from 5,400 to 4,500 years ago – but we can be reasonably confident that the two sites co-existed for much of their lives. The Stones of Stenness were probably erected shortly after people first came to live at Barnhouse.

The standing stones and henge would have looked very different when they were built and used. Centuries of ploughing have almost entirely removed the henge, or ceremonial enclosure, which once enclosed the standing stones.

The henge consisted of a substantial circular ditch (up to 4m wide and 2.3m deep) with an outer bank and a level platform at its centre.

On the north side, an 8m-wide causeway crossed the ditch, providing the only access to the centre. There were once at least 11 standing stones within the henge, forming an ellipse about 30m in diameter. Only four of the stones survive today, with the rest indicated by stumps and modern concrete markers.

The stones were probably erected over many years and may have been preceded by timber posts. Indeed, the process of erecting individual stones – and other events that took place here – may have been more significant than the completed monument itself.

Main image: A view of the stones from the south.

Opposite top: Photographs of visitors at site in 1909, with the 'dolmen' still in place.

Opposite bottom: The henge from the north-east, with the two 'dolmen' uprights foreground.

The hearth's significance is emphasised by a line of features marking the approach to it. Between the entrance to the henge and the hearth were a paved path, two stone settings, stone slabs that were apparently for another hearth, and the uprights of the 'dolmen'.

These features help indicate the complexity of the centre of the henge. This was a structured space to which access could be controlled, but people outside the site could see and hear activities in the centre.

The empty platform we see today may be misleading, but we can imagine a large fire at the centre, illuminating fingers of stone, and the sounds of people and musical instruments. Pottery and animal bones tell us that those who used the site were both cooking and eating here.

Our best guess is that the activities and ceremonies performed here marked the relationships between living and past communities, as well as with the natural world, and the passing of time.

DEBUNKING THE DOLMEN

Just inside the original entrance to the henge is an arrangement of smaller upright stones. Early accounts reported a very large, broad stone that lay towards the centre of the circle, and in his 1821 novel *The Pirate* Sir Walter Scott encouraged the idea that prehistoric Orcadians had used it as an altar for human sacrifice.

When the site came into State care in 1906, a 'dolmen' (a flat stone supported by vertical stones) was reconstructed in keeping with this interpretation. This 'dolmen' was removed in the mid-1970s, but the reconstruction had destroyed any surviving evidence of the original form.

CEREMONIAL USE

The focus of the interior is a large hearth, on the site of an earlier and smaller one. The earlier hearth was similar to the one underlying Structure 8 at Barnhouse. This suggests that the stone slabs from which it was made were brought here from Barnhouse.

Curiously, both this hearth and the one at Barnhouse had larger, more substantial hearths built right on top of them – these are the hearths that we see reconstructed today.

BETWEEN THE HENGES

In Neolithic times, there were more standing stones in this landscape than we see today. Those that still stand, coupled with the archaeological evidence, help us understand this unique ceremonial landscape.

Stenness comes from the Old Norse *stein-nes*, meaning 'stone promontory'. As well as standing stones, tombs and the massive ceremonial complex at the Ness of Brodgar, there were probably other Neolithic villages and monuments here.

Archaeologists believe that the standing stones in this area encouraged people to move in certain directions through the landscape. They may have marked significant routes or boundaries.

THE LOCHVIEW STONES

Two stones stand in front of a small house to the north of the isthmus. They are Neolithic, though little is known about their original context.

Above: A slightly exaggerated 18th-century illustration shows the Watchstone and the lost Odin Stone in the foreground with the Ring of Brodgar beyond.

Opposite top: The Lochview Stones.

Opposite bottom: The Watchstone, near the Stones of Stenness.

THE WATCHSTONE

The Watchstone is located beside the isthmus, a short distance from the Stones of Stenness. It stands more than 5.6m high.

It originally had a partner stone, which stood slightly to the south-west: its stump was found during roadworks in 1930. This stone and the Watchstone may once have marked the approach to the Ness of Brodgar.

THE ODIN STONE

The Odin Stone was another large standing stone close to the Stones of Stenness, with a distinctive hole through it. We have to rely on antiquarian accounts and drawings, as sadly it was destroyed in 1814. However, excavations in the 1990s, just north of the Stones of Stenness, revealed the probable spot where the Odin Stone stood.

THE BARNHOUSE STONE

The Barnhouse Stone stands alone in a field south of the isthmus. There has been no excavation here so we do not know whether it has always stood alone. It is located just 800m from Maeshowe and forms part of the midwinter solar alignment: the setting sun catches on the stone before shining into the chamber.

SOURCES OF STONE

The stones of the Stenness–Brodgar isthmus came from a number of different sources. Investigation of ancient quarries at Vestrafiold, north of Skara Brae, and at Staneyhill, north-east of the Loch of Harray, have given us an evocative insight into how the stones were quarried and transported.

At Vestrafiold, several broken monoliths survive in situ, together with evidence for the wedges and stone tools used to prise them from the bedrock. Once a stone had been quarried, it was dragged into position over a pit, which enabled the construction of a wooden raft beneath it. The stone was probably then secured to the raft to be transported for use.

The quarrying and transport of such huge stones must have involved a considerable amount of labour. Some have argued that the action of quarrying and erecting these stones was perhaps more significant than the final form of the standing stone or stone circle. Transport would certainly have been a task that brought many members of the community together.

HENGES AND STONE CIRCLES

Henges and stone circles are both thought to have been important places, where ceremonies may have been held, but they are distinct from each other. Standing stones and stone circles are often incorporated into henge monuments, but not all henges have standing stones and vice versa.

A henge is a circular or oval arena defined by a ditch and outer bank. Most henges have either one entrance or two at opposite sides. At the entrance, a causeway crosses the ditch, allowing access to the central area. Henges are found across the British Isles but none are recorded elsewhere.

We cannot be certain of the ideas, beliefs and practices associated with these monuments, but their relationship with the surrounding landscape was clearly important.

THE NESS OF BRODGAR

In 2002, geophysical survey of a low but extensive grassy mound on the Brodgar–Stenness isthmus provided the first glimpse of an extraordinary discovery.

The following year, the chance find of a large stone slab led to the first archaeological investigations on the site. Little was it known that this would lead to the unveiling of one of the most important archaeological sites found in the UK in recent years.

THE HEART OF NEOLITHIC ORKNEY?

The site has revealed evidence for a large complex of high-status stone buildings. The Ness of Brodgar was in use for over 1,000 years between 3500 and 2300 BC, during which it saw many phases of construction and alteration.

The location of the site suggests that it was particularly significant. It sits at the centre of a natural amphitheatre, between the other major ceremonial monuments, occupying the narrow neck of land between the Lochs of Harray and Stenness. It lies at the very heart of Neolithic Orkney.

It is clear that the Ness of Brodgar was not simply a village. So far no 'ordinary' house structures have been found here, but the buildings that have been excavated are impressive. The scale and quality of the stone architecture suggest something far from everyday. This impression is enhanced by the range and quality of artefacts found here.

In the late Neolithic, this complex would have dominated the Stenness–Brodgar landscape, and it may have been a focal point for communities across Orkney. Indeed, its influence may have extended beyond the islands, reversing the modern conception of Orkney as 'remote'.

The Ness of Brodgar was probably a ceremonial centre, perhaps a place of pilgrimage or a meeting place to celebrate important points in the year – at midwinter, for instance. It may also have been a place where religious or political leaders lived.

Archaeological excavation and research at the Ness of Brodgar is ongoing, led by the University of the Highlands and Islands Archaeology Institute and supported by the Ness of Brodgar Trust. We are only just beginning to understand this incredibly complex site.

Below: The Ness of Brodgar as it may have looked around 2850 BC. The large building at the centre is Structure 10. Beyond is the site of the Ring of Brodgar, which was probably not constructed until later.

As of 2017, the lowest levels of the site have not yet been reached, but they may provide vital clues as to why the site was chosen and how the Stenness–Brodgar area became such a significant focal point for ceremonial activity.

The Ness of Brodgar is a real treasure trove for archaeological analysis and understanding. It will not only add considerable depth to our understanding of Neolithic Orkney but also of developments in late Neolithic Britain in general.

UNDERSTANDING THE COMPLEX

At time of writing, the Ness of Brodgar is open for a short season of excavation each summer. Outside the excavation season, the site is carefully covered over to protect it from the elements.

To date, over 25 structures have been excavated at the Ness of Brodgar. The evidence suggests continual modification and enhancement throughout the life of the site. Successive buildings sit on top of earlier remains, indicating a very long period of use, and perhaps changing functions, over time.

A wide enclosure wall may have closed off the isthmus and served to separate the structures from the rest of the landscape. Individual features of the structures incorporate very similar elements to other late-Neolithic buildings such as the dwellings at Skara Brae, but the quality of the stonework and scale of construction lift them far beyond simple dwellings.

STRUCTURE 10

With its monumental proportions and elaborate entrance area, Structure 10 stands out from the others at the Ness (see illustration on previous page). It is far grander than any domestic structure and one of the largest Neolithic stone-built structures known in Britain.

Built around the same time as Structure 8 at Barnhouse (around 2900–2400 BC), Structure 10 incorporates features known from domestic houses, such as the angular recesses and dresser, but everything about it is on a much grander scale.

The free-standing dresser has been built with alternating red and yellow sandstone slabs. The exterior stonework has been very carefully built with finely dressed masonry. A huge amount of skill must have gone into the planning and construction of this building, and when complete it would have been unlike anything else in the Neolithic landscape.

Despite its grand outward appearance, the internal space is small. Structure 10 was designed to impress, but access to the interior was seemingly restricted to a select few.

Whatever its function, the eventual closure of Structure 10 was a momentous occasion. Excavations uncovered hundreds of cattle bones, including complete skulls, and whole deer carcasses, which had been laid carefully around the paved passageway surrounding the building. Archaeologists believe that the building may have been ritually 'decommissioned' with a huge feast, after which the animal remains were buried and the structure filled with midden (household waste).

A UNIQUE SITE

While the Ness of Brodgar is comparable to other late-Neolithic sites in many ways, its scale and degree of preservation distinguish it from them. Among the grand, finely built structures, a wealth of artefacts have been found on the site. Many of these are rare or high-status objects.

An extraordinary range of the style of pottery known as Grooved Ware has been found here, some of which is unique to the site. The fragments display a diverse variety of decoration, and evidence for different methods of manufacture, suggesting that visitors brought these pots from many different places.

Beautiful polished stone mace and axe heads have been found too, together with other curious carved stone objects. This suggests long-distance contacts and great skill in creating these items. The individuals who visited or used the site clearly had access to considerable resources.

Whether or not we ever understand precisely what went on at the Ness of Brodgar, it is clear that this was a very special place for the people of Neolithic Orkney.

Opposite: Archaeological investigations underway at the Ness of Brodgar.

Above, top to bottom: A selection of polished carved stone tools, decorated stonework and Grooved Ware pottery, all found at the site.

THE RING OF BRODGAR

At the northern end of the Brodgar isthmus, situated on a slight rise, is a second henge monument on a much grander scale than the Stones of Stenness.

The Ring of Brodgar is one of the most spectacular and well-preserved prehistoric monuments in Europe.

THE HENGE AND STONE CIRCLE

In contrast to the small henge at Stenness, with its single entrance, the Ring of Brodgar is one of the largest henge monuments in Britain. Its full extent, including its ditch, measures 130m, with two entrance causeways at opposite sides. The builders dug out the massive ditch in sections, quarrying it out of the bedrock – it would have been much deeper than it appears today.

Henge monuments are typically surrounded by an external bank, formed of material excavated from the ditch, but this is curiously absent from the Ring of Brodgar. Some of the material from the ditch presumably went to form the internal platform, but where the rest of it went remains a mystery.

The standing stones form a near perfect circle, measuring 104m in diameter, and 36 original stones survive from a total of up to 60. Thirteen of these were re-erected shortly after the monument came into State care in 1906, and another 13 survive as stumps. The stones come from a number of different sources, perhaps erected over time by different communities.

Below: An illustration of the Ring of Brodgar dated 1875.

We do not know whether the Neolithic builders ever finished erecting the 60 stones for which evidence was found, but there would certainly have been space for them.

RITUAL REMAINS

The Ring of Brodgar attracted interest from antiquarians from an early date. The earliest accounts go back to 1529, providing us with an invaluable early record of how the site looked then. But there has been very little archaeological investigation here, and there is much that we do not yet know.

We do not know what, if anything, was in the centre, or how this space may have been used. A report from the 1800s describes extensive turf-stripping at the site, and this may well mean that much archaeological evidence has been lost. Geophysical survey has provided little information, and only a small section of the monument has ever been excavated.

The limited scientific evidence we do have suggests that the henge was constructed sometime between 4,600 and 4,400 years ago. This would make it slightly later than the Stones of Stenness, which is perhaps the earliest henge in the British Isles.

As at Stenness, archaeologists think that the building and use of the Ring of Brodgar fulfilled social and ceremonial functions. Yet the Ring of Brodgar differs from the Stones of Stenness in terms of scale, layout and prominence in the landscape, suggesting that these two sites took on different roles or meanings to the communities that built and used them.

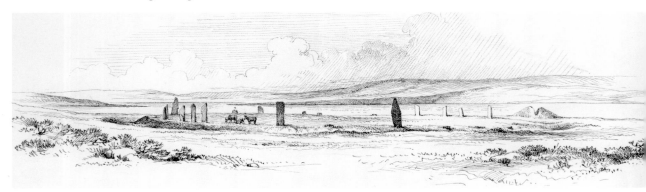

'They look like an assemblage of ancient Druids, mysteriously stern and invincibly silent and shaggy.'

Hugh Miller Scottish geologist, on his visit to the Ring of Brodgar in 1846

Above: A view of the Ring of Brodgar from the south-west, with the Loch of Harray beyond.

MONUMENTS AROUND THE RING OF BRODGAR

Many visitors today appreciate the Ring of Brodgar for the 'natural' and wild quality of its setting, though humans have stamped their mark all over this landscape.

The Ring of Brodgar is more than a stone circle and henge. It also provides a focus for other standing stones, and for many Neolithic and Bronze Age burial mounds that survive on both sides of the modern road.

The most recent may date to 3,500 years ago, but the earliest may pre-date the Ring of Brodgar and help to explain its existence. Though many have not survived the depredations of more recent agriculture, the number, scale and diversity of those that survive tell us that people regarded the area as important for a long time, and continued to use the Ring as a focus for ceremonial activities for many centuries.

Besides the mounds described below, at least eight other small mounds lie to the south of the Ring. From some angles they are nearly invisible, but keep an eye out for them. From the pathway around the RSPB reserve, they can be seen as an impressive group on the skyline. Some of the mounds around the Ring have been disturbed by antiquarian diggings, but few discoveries have been reported.

SALT KNOWE

The most prominent of the mounds surrounding the Ring lies just a short distance away to the south-west. Its name is thought to come from its location, next to the saltwater Loch of Stenness, as distinguished from Fresh Knowe adjacent to the freshwater Loch of Harray.

This massive mound, measuring 40m by 6m, is comparable in scale to Maeshowe. The date of its construction and its function remain a mystery. It was once thought to contain a stone chamber similar to that at Maeshowe, but historic investigations and geophysical survey have failed to provide evidence for internal structures.

Above: The Ring of Brodgar and surrounding monuments.

Right: Soapstone urn found inside one of Plumcake Mound's two cists, or stone coffins.

SOUTH KNOWE

The depression at the top of this mound shows that it has been disturbed in the past. We know it was investigated in the 1800s, but there are no reports of any discoveries. If you look carefully, you can see the line of an old track that ran between South Knowe and the Ring of Brodgar.

COMET STONE

The Comet Stone is a 1.75m-high standing stone south-east of the Ring of Brodgar. It was originally part of a group of similar stones, and you can see two stumps rising from the low mound on which it stands.

This may have been an important point in the landscape for viewing and experiencing the ceremonial sites. Folklore surrounds the stone, including the story that it was once a giant fiddler, turned to stone.

It is certainly a good place to take in your surroundings today. Look out for the low bank running from the south towards the mound and then on to Plumcake Mound – an example of later field boundaries which have been aligned along existing features in the landscape.

FRESH KNOWE

Antiquarian James Farrer dug a trench across the north end of this mound in 1853. He observed the mound had been carefully constructed, but reported no other finds. Fresh Knowe's elliptical shape and large size suggest it might be a Neolithic burial mound that pre-dates the Ring of Brodgar.

PLUMCAKE MOUND

Named for its shape, Plumcake Mound is slightly smaller than the nearby Fresh Knowe. When Farrer and his fellow antiquarian George Petrie dug the mound in 1854 they found two stone cists. One contained a decorated steatite (soapstone) urn, the other a pottery urn, both holding cremated human remains and both likely to post-date the Ring.

Top left: Plumcake Mound.

Top right: Salt Knowe, on a similar scale to Maeshowe, though no evidence of an internal structure has been discovered.

Bottom right: The Comet Stone, south-east of the Ring of Brodgar, perhaps once part of a group of standing stones.

THE NATURAL SETTING

The Ring of Brodgar sits within spectacular natural surroundings, which must have contributed to the selection of the site.

You can walk all around the site, but it will help to protect the fragile ecosystem if you keep to the mown paths and do not climb the mounds. From the Ring you can take a circular route through land owned by the RSPB.

The site can also be reached on foot from the Stones of Stenness, where you can join the footpath by Brodgar Farm. This longer path takes you past the Ness of Brodgar and alongside the Lochs of Harray and Stenness, giving you a better feel for this ancient landscape. Allow around an hour to enjoy this route. If you're lucky you can experience the local wildlife, as well as very different views of how the monuments sit in the landscape.

NATURE CONSERVATION

Maintaining the Ring of Brodgar involves keeping the vegetation as natural as possible and managing the grassland to encourage wild flowers and breeding birds. Since 2001 the RSPB has managed the farmland encircling the site. This includes maintaining a semi-natural wetland north of the Ring to encourage more breeding waders and wintering wildfowl, and ensuring that the arable area immediately outside the Ring promotes farmland biodiversity.

Birds visiting the area include waders, skylarks, finches, buntings and hen harriers. Animal and insect life is abundant too, from brown hares to great yellow bumblebees and the elusive Orkney vole.

The arable weeds that grow in the area would be recognised by our ancestors. They include purple ramping fumitory, traditionally used as a medicinal herb, and fat hen, which could be cultivated as a grain. This vegetation gives us an idea of how the land looked in Neolithic times. As today, there would have been primroses in the spring and wild orchids, heather and bell heather during the summer months.

Top: A lapwing, one of the species found in the area close to the Ring of Brodgar managed by the RSPB.

Above: A bumblebee, another species often seen in the area.

Opposite: Sandstone cliffs near Skara Brae.

BOOKAN: ANOTHER CEREMONIAL FOCUS?

North-west of the Ring of Brodgar there is another cluster of archaeological sites. Most are visible from the Ring of Brodgar or the road, but recent geophysical surveys have illuminated the variety and extent of archaeology still hidden underground.

The Ring of Bookan stands a short distance north-west of the Ring of Brodgar, concealed just behind the brow of a hill. Here, a large circular ditch encloses a central area which appears at one time to have included a chamber.

Close to this is another large mound called Skae Frue. In the mid-1800s, this was dug into by antiquarians, who found three cists containing human bones.

There are other mounds around the Ring of Bookan, but perhaps the most intriguing is Bookan Chambered Cairn on the slopes below. The cairn survives only as a low mound today, but it would once have been much more substantial, commanding views south over the Brodgar isthmus.

In 2002 archaeologists excavated the site to advance the knowledge gained from excavations in 1861 by Farrer and Petrie. They found that the cairn had a much more complicated history of development than Farrer recognised. It is originally late Neolithic in date and was embellished towards the end of its development to create a much grander monument.

In the wider landscape many more burial mounds can be found, including the rare survival of a 'disc barrow' at Wasbister, which probably contained a cist at its centre. Many of these burial mounds are thought to date from the Bronze Age. They appear to respect the earlier Neolithic ceremonial sites, suggesting that the area was significant for a long period of time, even as society and beliefs changed.

FIELD SYSTEMS AND SETTLEMENT

The landscape around Bookan and Brodgar also reveals tantalising evidence for human settlement and agriculture, dating from at least the Bronze Age to more recent times.

An earthen bank known as the Dyke o' Sean snakes its way between the lochs of Harray and Stenness. Today it comprises the boundary between the parishes of Stenness and Sandwick.

During the early Bronze Age (around 4,500 years ago) there was a move towards the enclosure of land and the development of more permanent field systems – the dyke may date to the division of land at this time.

Elsewhere, there are traces of prehistoric houses. At Wasbister, you can just make out the remains of a house, which survives as the low, stony foundations of two conjoined circular structures. To the surprise of archaeologists, geophysical survey has revealed that this house sits within four hectares of fields and other traces of settlement. These remains are likely to date to the Bronze Age, but a Neolithic date has not yet been ruled out.

Opposite: The Ring of Bookan, about a mile north-west of the Ring of Brodgar. The smaller mound to its west is Skara Frue.

Top left: Wasbister Barrow.

Top right: Wasbister House.

Right: Broken mace-heads found at Bookan.

SKARA BRAE

> 'A place that touches the heart… a cluster of houses where we can see that people moved and lived and loved.'
>
> **George Mackay Brown**, *Portrait of Orkney* (1981)

On the west coast of the Orkney mainland, about 5 miles (9km) from the Ring of Brodgar, lies the best-preserved prehistoric farming settlement in northern Europe.

Skara Brae was continuously inhabited for around 600 years, from approximately 3100 BC to 2500 BC, around the time when the Stones of Stenness, Maeshowe and the Ring of Brodgar were constructed and in use.

The village survives in exceptionally good condition because of the quality of its construction and because it was buried by sand shortly after abandonment. As a result, it provides us with an extraordinary insight into Neolithic life.

BURIAL AND DISCOVERY

Skara Brae was originally built next to a small inland loch, but over the centuries the land between Skara Brae and the sea disappeared due to coastal erosion. The village was then buried beneath sand dunes, but this seems to have occurred long after settlement here had ended. Skara Brae is no Orcadian Pompeii.

The site was first discovered in 1850, after a storm stripped the grass from the coastal dunes. Curious antiquarians explored the site, but its present appearance owes much to the clearance and consolidation of the site between 1928 and 1930 by the archaeologist Gordon Childe. Childe's primary motivation was to present the site to the public after it came into State care.

Below: House 1 at Skara Brae, with typical layout of hearth, bed enclosures and 'dresser'.

DIFFERENT PHASES

We will never know how large the settlement at Skara Brae was, as we cannot be sure how much of it has been lost to the sea. Nor can we fully understand its complex history. However, all the evidence suggests a community of people who lived and worked closely together.

Visitors to Skara Brae will see two distinct phases displayed, but the reality was much more organic, as houses were built, altered, abandoned and replaced by new structures.

The houses at Skara Brae were built in close proximity to one another. The earlier houses were freestanding, with paths between them.

Later houses were built over these, and were deliberately dug into earlier midden, which provided stability and insulation.

Towards the end of the period of occupation, as the coast encroached ever closer and conditions worsened, the passages between houses were roofed over with great slabs to provide shelter. This gave early archaeologists the false idea that Skara Brae was subterranean.

While all of the houses share the same basic form, the later buildings are slightly larger and had stone fittings (interpreted as beds) that projected into the central space, instead of being built into the walls. Each house included one or more cells built into the walls, a central hearth, and stone-built 'dresser' opposite the entrance.

Above: Skara Brae as it may have looked when inhabited.

UNDERSTANDING THE BUILDINGS

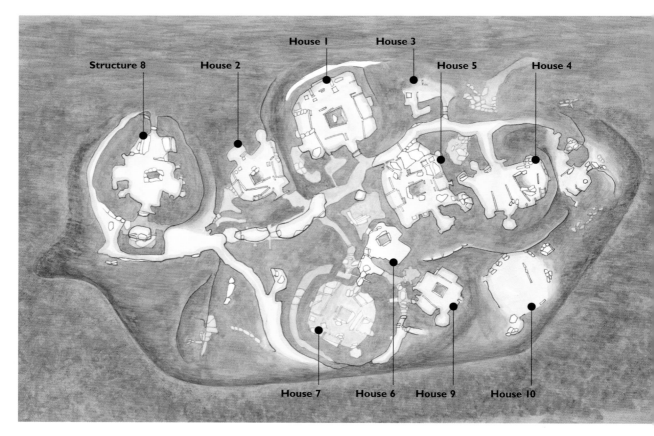

The well-preserved remains of Skara Brae help us to imagine what Barnhouse Village and other settlements may once have looked like.

This is not to suggest that the architecture of the villages, or the people who lived in them, were identical. Nonetheless, there are similarities in the architecture and the use of buildings at Skara Brae, Barnhouse and other settlements, such as Links of Noltand on the island of Westray, that hint at a common way of doing things. A far better range of artefacts has survived at Skara Brae than at Barnhouse, allowing us more insight into the lives of its residents.

Top: The surviving structures at Skara Brae. Visitors can now view these from a paved walkway (not shown). Areas shown in pale green are covered over.

Right: The interior of a Skara Brae house as it may have looked when in use.

Top: House 9, one of the two visible structures from the earlier phase of development.

Above: Neolithic carvings discovered on one of the partitions in House 7.

Below: Bone jewellery – examples of the thousands of artefacts found at the site.

HOUSE 9

This is a good example of one of the freestanding houses from the earlier phase of building at Skara Brae, with its 'beds' built into the core of the wall. It is similar to House 3 at Barnhouse. The houses from the earlier building phases are less well preserved than those that came later. The builders of the later dwellings probably robbed these houses for materials, which they reused in their new constructions.

HOUSE 1

This is one of the largest and best preserved houses at Skara Brae. It is later than House 9, and illustrates the classic arrangement of box 'beds' and a dresser around a central hearth. Around the hearth are stone querns for grinding cereals, as well as tanks for food or bait storage. It is worth noting that the small window to the right of the dresser was inserted during early consolidation work by William Watt, who discovered the site.

HOUSE 7

This house has several unusual features setting it apart from the rest of Skara Brae. It stood further back and, unlike the other houses, its door could only be locked from the outside. It is also notable for the great quantity of incised stone decoration found inside and for the burials of two women found beneath its floor. The distinctive qualities and use of this building evoke House 2 at Barnhouse.

STRUCTURE 8

This building was also set apart from the others and seems to have had a different function, possibly as a workshop. Its internal layout differs from the houses, with no stone beds or dresser. When it was excavated, its floor was covered with fragments of pottery and chert, a flint-like stone from which prehistoric tools were made. Structure 8 reminds us of House 6 at Barnhouse, which was lived in but was also the focus of stone-working.

ABOUT NEOLITHIC ORKNEY

The rich ceremonial and settlement remains of Neolithic Orkney provide us with a great wealth of evidence for a dynamic period of our past.

These monuments, along with numerous other Neolithic sites across Orkney, provide an exceptional insight into the first farming communities in Scotland.

The people who built them were not Orkney's first inhabitants. From the limited evidence we have, it seems people first explored Orkney some 13,000 years ago, though the islands were probably first occupied around 9,000 years ago. These early settlers were hunter-gatherers, who moved from place to place, living off seasonally available plants, as well as hunting and fishing. Discoveries of flint tools provide fascinating glimpses into how they lived.

Things began to change around 6,000 years ago, with the adoption of farming. New settlers came to Orkney from the mainland of Scotland, bringing domesticated animals and seeds.

These people were the first to settle in permanent villages and build lasting monuments. With this new way of life came new beliefs.

EARLY SETTLERS

The earliest evidence of settled communities that we have on mainland Orkney comes from sites such as Wideford, Stonehall and Smerquoy around the Bay of Firth near Finstown. Some of the earliest houses were built of wood, but gradually stone buildings came to replace these earlier timber structures, perhaps as more woodland was cleared to make way for cultivation.

In addition to individual farmsteads, such as the Knap of Howar on the island of Papa Westray, some communities lived in small villages, like that recently found at Smerquoy.

By around 3800 BC these early farming communities were becoming established; it was these communities that built the houses, tombs, henges and standing stones that survive today.

This page: The Ring of Brodgar.

MARKING TIME
AND PLACE

As these early farming communities established a new relationship with the land, their perceptions of time and place changed and developed.

Tombs, henges, stone circles and other massive stone structures are among the earliest attempts by our ancestors to make a permanent mark on the landscape. The Neolithic stonemasons of Orkney built to impress through physical form, texture, scale and architectural finesse.

These huge ceremonial monuments were deliberately and carefully located in the landscape. Precise calculations were made to create viewpoints and alignments between the monuments, with the wider landscape, and with the heavens.

Some are virtually invisible from certain viewpoints, but from others they rise out of the landscape to confront us with their presence. The builders thought carefully about how to achieve such effects.

The henge, platform and standing stones at the Ring of Brodgar form a prominent landscape feature, particularly if seen from the Loch of Harray side. The builders may also have been mimicking features of the surrounding landscape.

PURPOSE AND MOVEMENT

In Neolithic Orkney, as in modern times, social practice and architecture conditioned where people could go and what they experienced. This is reflected in the built remains: tombs and henges, villages and houses. Considerable effort went into separating spaces from each other and placing restrictions on those who might enter.

Henges were constructed in a way that would control the movement of people. The alignment of the henge entrances in Orkney suggests the importance of directing people between the Stones of Stenness to the south and the Ring of Bookan to the north.

At the heart of this landscape was the ceremonial complex of the Ness of Brodgar. Everyone who passed along this routeway through the landscape would have had to follow a prescribed route, and all would have encountered those who were active at Barnhouse and the Ness of Brodgar.

The discovery of this ceremonial complex has led us to rethink the significance and function of the surrounding monuments. We must now consider their combined role in a dramatic architecture that defined movement and activity throughout this landscape.

DOMESTIC ORDER

Barnhouse and Skara Brae also show the importance of form, orientation and location for Neolithic Orcadians. The architecture of later Neolithic dwellings is noticeably uniform across Orkney. Almost all of the structures have similar internal arrangements, with a central hearth, beds to each side, and a 'dresser' at the rear. This broad uniformity suggests a certain order in domestic life and shared beliefs within society.

The similarity between the dwellings has suggested to some that society may have been largely egalitarian. However, as the Neolithic developed, signs emerged of a more stratified society, including more architecturally distinct structures, on a much grander scale and with very finely built walls and often more elaborate layouts. These hint at changes in society and beliefs.

At Barnhouse there is a sense that the buildings are set around an open space, where people gathered for activities.

The arrangement of buildings and the traces of activities left behind suggests an ordering of space, with different areas set aside for different functions at both domestic and ceremonial sites.

We can never know how these early people viewed the world, but they are likely to have been sensitive to the passing of the seasons; the cycles of the Moon and the Sun may have been particularly important. Aspects of these beliefs are apparent in their architecture.

This architecture provided one important way by which the people of Neolithic Orkney could structure and transform their environment. Through it they were able to subtly demonstrate their world views and create or maintain social order, just as we do today.

Opposite: An illustration of 1772 by John Cleveley shows the relationship between the Stones of Stenness (foreground), the Odin Stone (right), the Watchstone (centre) and the Ring of Brodgar (in the distance).

Above: Maeshowe within its bowl-shaped setting.

DEATH AND BURIAL

The chambered tombs of the Neolithic suggest attitudes to death and burial that were very different from those of today.

The bones of the dead were laid within these massive stone tombs, but the evidence suggests that not everyone from the community was buried in this way. Nor were these places reserved solely for the dead. They were designed to be accessed and reused by the living.

Many were used over several centuries, with new bones interred periodically and earlier remains sometimes cleared out or rearranged. Great care seems to have been taken to arrange the bones: in some tombs the remains are grouped into skulls or long bones.

The bodies of the ancestors seem to have played an important part in the daily life of Scotland's prehistoric peoples.

A SENSE OF BELONGING

The assertion of ancestral connections to a particular place was common to most prehistoric societies, including Neolithic Orkney. With the adoption of farming, people became tied to the land, as houses and the surrounding land were used over many generations.

Communal tombs provided a very visible way to associate a local community with a given area, weaving the remains of the dead into the fabric of daily life.

There are other aspects of life that may also have held similar significance. The moving and recycling of hearthstones suggests that these, too, held a meaning beyond the simple generation of fire. It may have been closely associated with particular groups of people and their specific geographical place.

Standing stones may have been associated with individuals: iconic representations both of the places from which they came, and of those who transported them.

It may not be unreasonable to imagine these standing stones as monumental representations of human forms, positioned in the landscape as a way of linking memory and ancestry to the land.

Polished stone maceheads also seem to have a ritual significance and possible associations with the dead. Many show signs of deliberate breakage and burial, perhaps representing the death of an individual or even a group identity.

SHARED ARCHITECTURE

Parallels in the architecture of Orcadian late Neolithic houses and Maeshowe-type tombs reinforce the sense of an ever-present relationship between the living and the dead.

At Barnhouse, the design and orientation of later buildings may have reflected daily and annual life cycles. Similarly, Maeshowe is intimately associated with the birth of each new year, or death of the last.

The outer enclosure of Barnhouse's Structure 8 faces Maeshowe, while the entrance to its internal building aligns on the midsummer sunset, the seasonal opposite of Maeshowe. Such references and oppositions surely carried great and intentional symbolic meaning.

Above: Artist's impression of a burial ritual in Neolithic Orkney.

Opposite: The interior of Cuween Hill Chambered Cairn, about 3 miles (5km) south-west of Maeshowe.

BUILDING IN STONE

Nature blessed Orkney's Neolithic inhabitants with a landscape formed of Old Red Sandstone. This is an excellent building material that readily forms into plentiful, regular-shaped slabs.

This is also a blessing for us today, trying to understand Neolithic Orkney. Many prehistoric structures survive here because people mastered the art of drystone masonry, learning to square the edges and smooth the surfaces of stones, without metal tools or machinery.

The great architectural achievement of Maeshowe and the finely built structures at the Ness of Brodgar stand as a testament to the skill of these early stone masons. Selection of stone required a detailed understanding of both geology and masonry. The more rounded stones used at settlements near the coast, such as Skara Brae, suggest that some stone could be collected from the beach.

Stone for construction at Barnhouse and the Ness of Brodgar may have also been available locally, in outcrops along the sides of the lochs that were later submerged as the loch levels rose.

For the great standing stones, Neolithic architects looked further afield to quarries such as Vestrafiold and Staneyhill. This may have been partly due to the necessity of finding slabs of a suitable hardness and size, but it is also thought to reflect the spread of the Neolithic community across Orkney.

Once a stone had been extracted from the quarries, it might be shaped, and then it had to be transported to the site where it would be erected. This must have been a phenomenal exercise. Not only were the stones potentially breakable, but there was also the sheer strength necessary to move them across land. Several possible solutions have been suggested, such as the use of rope and rollers, or sleds, the provision of seaweed as a lubricant, or the possibility that they may have been transported by boat.

Some estimates suggest it took as many as 80,000 man-hours to build the Ring of Brodgar, and up to 50,000 man-hours to erect the Stones of Stenness. The amount of labour required, combined with the likelihood that the stones at the Ring of Brodgar come from different locations, suggests that multiple communities were involved in the construction.

There is no evidence of a centralised authority in Neolithic Orkney, but the creation and use of these monuments certainly required centralised planning and people with a long-term vision. They also indicate that society was able (and willing) to set aside time and resources in addition to the simple tasks of everyday farming.

Below: Knap of Howar on the Orkney island of Papa Westray is northern Europe's oldest surviving dwelling.

NEOLITHIC ART

Below: i. Lozenge-shaped carving found at Skara Brae, ii. Decorated slab found at Pierowall on the island of Westray, iii. Stone decorated with pigments found at the Ness of Brodgar.

Bottom: Carved stone objects found at Skara Brae.

Decorated stonework has been recorded at many Neolithic sites across Orkney. The discovery of hundreds of incised stones at the Ness of Brodgar has led to much more research into the meaning and significance of Neolithic art.

Artwork has been found at domestic sites, chambered tombs and ceremonial sites. Most of this is carved stone, in a range of forms. Incised lines, simple abstract patterns, chevrons and zig-zags are most common, but curvilinear motifs, spirals and peck-marks have also been found.

Today, we have to look hard to recognise these carvings. Surprisingly, they were often created on surfaces that would later be covered by other courses of stone. It seems that the act of incising the stone was just as important as the motif and it is unlikely that they were designed to be read in the way that we traditionally think of art.

The people who created this work were clearly using a repertoire of designs to communicate something but, so far, it has proved impossible for us to decipher it.

The art at Skara Brae, Maeshowe and Ness of Brodgar has been closely studied. We can only speculate as to how many more carvings remain to be discovered at other sites.

Some of the stonework was also painted. At the Ness of Brodgar there is evidence for red and yellow paint made from ochre and haematite, and at Skara Brae small stone pots with traces of pigments were found. The bare stone buildings that survive today may have looked quite different in the Neolithic.

Decoration is also found on a rich variety of the objects from these sites. The angular and curvilinear designs on Grooved Ware pots are comparable to many of the designs on the stonework.

At Skara Brae, unusual carved stone objects were found which perhaps had a special function. The time and effort invested in their meticulous working – coupled with the fact that the stone used is imported, not native – suggest that these were high-status objects and used in very specific, perhaps restricted, ways.

In 2009, excavations at Links of Noltland on the island of Westray discovered a small stone figurine of a woman. The 'Westray Wife' or 'Orkney Venus' is the earliest representation of the human form in Britain. Examples of figurative Neolithic art are very rare, but the recognition of this figure led to discoveries of other figurines, including the re-discovery of a piece from Skara Brae that had been long forgotten.

We may never fully understand the meaning behind these decorations and carved stone objects, but they give us a rare insight into a rich and colourful world.

DAY-TO-DAY LIVING

From Skara Brae, Barnhouse and other Neolithic structures we can begin to construct a picture of daily life in Neolithic Orkney.

The midden material – household rubbish – from around the settlements provides us with a remarkable insight into the diet and economy of these communities.

The architecture of the villages gives the impression of a sophisticated lifestyle: houses had central hearths, stone furniture, insulation from surrounding midden material and complex drainage systems. The wealth of surviving prehistoric material in Orkney allows us a much better understanding of everyday life than is possible elsewhere in Scotland.

NATURAL RESOURCES

Unlike their neighbours in mainland Scotland, ancient Orcadians were fortunate to have no animal predators and competitors to contend with, such as wolves and bears.

Their main challenge was ensuring that food was available at all times, and especially when the crops failed. Archaeological evidence tells us that they exploited a diverse range of both domestic and wild resources.

Cattle and sheep were more than a source of meat – they also provided milk, blood, skins, wool and bone for working into tools and other objects. Evidence suggests that when animals were slaughtered, the messy process of butchery took place away from the main settlements. Towards the end of the period there is evidence that cattle may have become prized possessions, important as a source of wealth and wellbeing, in addition to their value as food.

Orkney's Neolithic farmers also fished, hunted and gathered. As well as fish and shellfish, communities made use of whales and other marine mammals. Their hides served as an excellent source of oil for lamps and their bones for tools, utensils and building materials.

Wild birds were useful for meat, eggs and oil, while red deer, now extinct on Orkney, were an excellent source of leather, bone and antler for tools such as picks, as well as meat. Early Orcadians cultivated cereals, such as barley and wheat, and collected hazelnuts, edible wild seeds and fruit, including crab apples and crowberries.

Analysis of Grooved Ware pottery suggests some vessels were used for cooking plants and milk-related products. Bone and stone tools suggest a wide range of craft activities, including leather, stone and woodworking. Not all objects are obviously utilitarian: some would have been used in games while others are likely to have had ritual significance.

HEARTHS AND HEALTH

Hearths were an important source of light and warmth and they formed the central focus of Neolithic dwellings. They may have had a symbolic role too, as a source of life with the power to transform. Outside the home, hearths played a role in communal feasting and possibly in symbolic purification at the entrance to a special place. A range of materials might be used as fuel, including driftwood, turf, animal dung, dried seaweed and heather.

We have no evidence for what Neolithic people wore – presumably leathers, skins and felted fabrics (there is no evidence of weaving). We know that bone pins, beads and pendants formed adornments. People may have used coloured pigments to decorate their bodies and clothes, along with feathers (which could also be used for insulation).

Knowledge of the benefits and dangers of certain plants will have developed from earliest times. For instance, a large quantity of puffballs found at Skara Brae suggests that its inhabitants recognised the fungus's medicinal value in helping to clot blood.

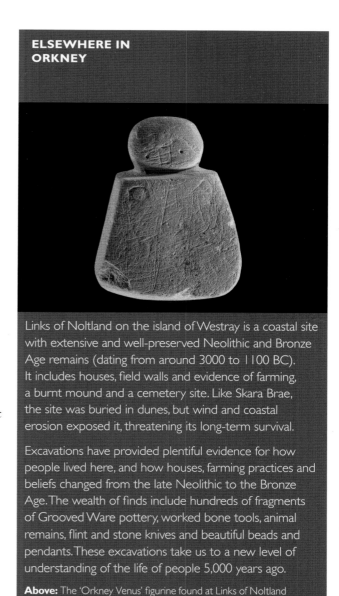

ELSEWHERE IN ORKNEY

Links of Noltland on the island of Westray is a coastal site with extensive and well-preserved Neolithic and Bronze Age remains (dating from around 3000 to 1100 BC). It includes houses, field walls and evidence of farming, a burnt mound and a cemetery site. Like Skara Brae, the site was buried in dunes, but wind and coastal erosion exposed it, threatening its long-term survival.

Excavations have provided plentiful evidence for how people lived here, and how houses, farming practices and beliefs changed from the late Neolithic to the Bronze Age. The wealth of finds include hundreds of fragments of Grooved Ware pottery, worked bone tools, animal remains, flint and stone knives and beautiful beads and pendants. These excavations take us to a new level of understanding of the life of people 5,000 years ago.

Above: The 'Orkney Venus' figurine found at Links of Noltland on the island of Westray.

Left: Artist's impression of Skara Brae residents decorating pots.

Right: Puffball fungi of the kind used at Skara Brae, probably for medicinal purposes.

BEYOND ORKNEY

This major ceremonial landscape at the heart of Neolithic Orkney suggests the emergence of a sophisticated and hierarchical society in Orkney by the late Neolithic period.

The henge monuments at the Ring of Brodgar and Stones of Stenness and the ceremonial centre at the Ness of Brodgar are likely to have been a focal point for communities across the whole of Orkney and possibly beyond.

ORCADIAN ORIGINS?

The preservation of Neolithic remains in Orkney is exceptional, but these sites and the traditions and beliefs that they represent are not unique.

Across Britain and Ireland, Neolithic people did many things in very similar ways. Defining activities included the burial of the dead in communal tombs, the construction of henges, the erection of timber and stone circles, the conspicuous production of high-status objects and the use of Grooved Ware – a distinctive form of pottery with incised and applied decoration.

Current dating evidence suggests that the development of these traditions and beliefs may have had their origins in Orkney. The Stones of Stenness may be the earliest henge monument in Britain, and early examples of Grooved Ware pots have been found at Links of Noltland and the Ness of Brodgar.

Similar complexes of ceremonial monuments exist at Newgrange in Ireland's Boyne Valley, and in southern England at Stonehenge and Avebury. Comparable designs have been found on Grooved Ware at these sites, as have ornate stone objects and carvings on tombs and houses. All of this reinforces the connection.

These traditions did not arise in Orkney out of the blue. Archaeological evidence indicates that farming arrived here some 6,000 years ago. The fertile local conditions meant that people could settle and society could develop. Architectural differences between earlier structures and those of the later Neolithic may mark the rise of more complex social conditions. These could have led to the development of new styles of house, artefacts such as pottery, and belief systems.

Above: Map of Britain and Ireland showing major Neolithic monuments. There is strong evidence of contact between them.

Above: Avebury in Wiltshire, site of a Neolithic henge containing three circles of standing stones.

Top: Stonehenge, also in Wiltshire. It may have been built after the Stones of Stenness.

SEAFARING FOLK

By 2500 BC the ceremonial landscape on the Orkney mainland had reached its peak. At that time the ceremonial complex of sites on the Stenness–Brodgar isthmus may have been a focal point for communities from far and wide.

Orkney occupies a pivotal maritime location, at the top of the British mainland. This may help to explain its significance – and the strong links that exist between its architecture, pottery and carvings and those elsewhere in Britain and Ireland. Neolithic Orkney was a seafaring society with far-reaching contacts. No vessels survive from this time, but we should imagine skin boats capable of carrying people and animals.

The discovery of exotic artefacts in Orkney also speaks of distant connections. Some of the distinctive stone used to create the beautifully polished mace and axe heads from these sites came from quarries on the Isle of Arran and in the Lake District in north-west England. Objects and ideas must have flowed in and out of Orkney over considerable distances.

FROM THEN TO NOW

In the Neolithic and early Bronze Age the Stenness–Brodgar area was an outstanding place, clearly special to the communities of Britain. However, there came a point when the use of the monuments changed radically.

Eventually, people no longer entered Maeshowe or used it for burial. They also altered, or stopped altogether, their ceremonies at the Stones of Stenness and Ring of Brodgar. But hundreds of subsequent generations continued to shape the land and add to the rich history of these islands.

The area around the Ring of Brodgar, with its burial mounds, suggests that ritual activity continued – perhaps a reflection of the continuing importance of the area. Iron Age sites such as the probable broch at Big Howe, near the Stones of Stenness, were also placed close to earlier centres of importance.

Many centuries later, Norsemen established churches, meeting places and farmsteads in the land around Maeshowe. Their tales, and the rich record of runic graffiti they have left inside the mound, demonstrate the important role that Maeshowe continued to play for them.

Across Orkney, a body of folklore developed to explain the monuments, such as tales of the trows (trolls) who lived in the mounds, and many of these stories are still told today.

In more recent centuries, farming has dominated the area's history and appearance. Many early discoveries in Orkney were made as a result of farming, as earlier stone monuments were revealed by the plough. Today, archaeology, heritage and tourism have helped drive the way we manage and use this area.

Below: 'General Plan of the Antiquities of Stenness', produced by Captain F.W.L. Thomas in 1849.

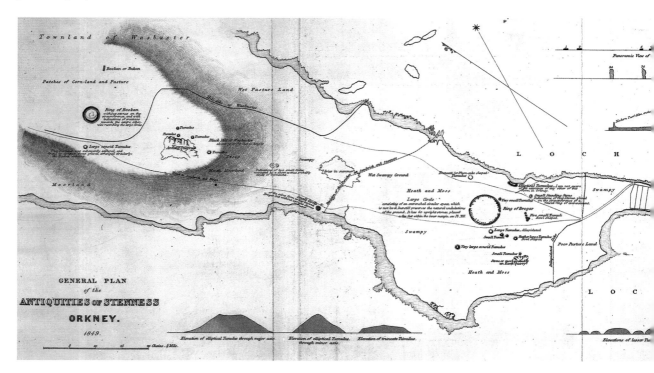

ANTIQUARIAN INTEREST

The task of unpicking the landscape around Maeshowe begins with the records left to us by antiquarians – those forerunners of modern archaeologists, who sought to understand the ancient world.

Some of the earliest records of these sites come from detailed plans by Sir Joseph Banks (1772) and Sir John Thomas Stanley (1789). Their surveys and sketches are systematic and show a good eye for detail.

Investigations flourished in the 1800s. Maeshowe and the Stenness–Brodgar area attracted considerable antiquarian interest, and people such as James Farrer, George Petrie and Sir Henry Dryden were all drawn to try their hands at excavation.

They left plans, drawings and accounts of their work here, but unfortunately their excavation techniques and records were poor by modern standards, so it is impossible to interpret their findings in detail.

They do provide us with some important clues and alert us to the archaeological possibilities of Orkney's monumental landscape, but they lack the precision required by today's archaeologists.

One benefit of this early interest, however, was that it led to Orkney's monuments being among the first in Britain to become legally protected.

Right: An illustration of the interior of Maeshowe by James Farrer, who rediscovered it in 1861.

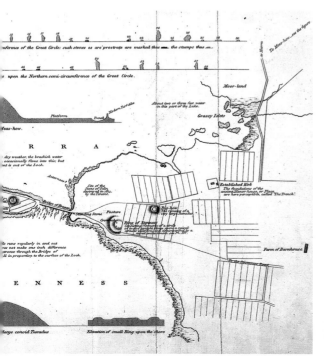

MODERN DISCOVERIES

Orkney's monuments have long had an important role in the development of archaeological thought.

During the 20th century our knowledge of archaeology and prehistory improved dramatically, allowing us to make firmer assumptions about the Neolithic monuments in Orkney and elsewhere.

Today, we take it for granted that the buildings that make up the World Heritage Site date from the Neolithic period, more than 5,000 years ago. But when Gordon Childe, a founding father of archaeology, excavated Skara Brae in the 1920s he declared it to be Pictish – dating from around 1,300 years ago – rather than Neolithic. Even in the 1930s, when Childe realised he was wrong, he had no way to provide a scientific date for the site.

RADIOCARBON REVOLUTION

The biggest leap forward in understanding prehistoric buildings and artefacts came with the radiocarbon revolution of the 1950s, allowing for the scientific dating of archaeological sites and objects.

Our knowledge about Orkney's Neolithic monuments is still limited, however. The present dates for the World Heritage Site largely derive from small-scale excavations in the 1970s. In the surrounding area, the results from more recent scientific excavations at Barnhouse, Stonehall and Wideford have now been fully published.

On the monuments which form the World Heritage Site, there has been relatively little excavation to modern standards. Where small trenches have been opened in order to answer specific questions, such as the date of the ditch at the Ring of Brodgar, it has often proved surprisingly difficult to get the answers we seek. One problem lies in the fact that excavation itself is a destructive process.

WORLD HERITAGE RESEARCH

Nevertheless, it important to understand the landscape and lives of the World Heritage sites, and to set them into their proper context in Neolithic Orkney. For this reason, research continues across the wider area around the monuments.

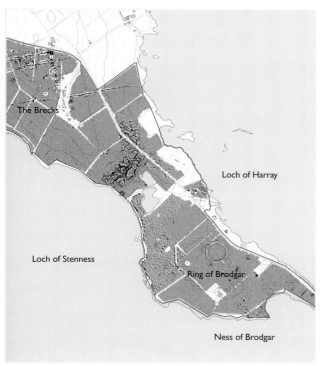

The Brecks

Loch of Harray

Loch of Stenness

Ring of Brodgar

Ness of Brodgar

Investigations around the Bay of Firth have uncovered evidence for early timber buildings on several sites, as well as further stone settlements. Analysis of these is helping to fill out the details of Neolithic society.

Non-invasive methods of surveying and recording, such as geophysics, enable us to understand the landscape better, and to monitor and conserve the monuments more effectively.

Geophysical surveys have taken place across much of the World Heritage Site, providing valuable information about the landscape and surviving buried remains. More recently, a programme of laser scanning has produced an exceptionally accurate record of all of the upstanding monuments, revealing evidence for previously unrecorded details at sites such as Maeshowe.

These investigations have been complemented by the large-scale excavations at the Ness of Brodgar and at Links of Noltland (see page 57).

New techniques and scientific developments also allow artefacts and human remains from earlier excavations to be studied in a new light, allowing us to fine-tune our understanding of Orkney's prehistory.

Orkney continues to surprise and transform our understanding of Neolithic times. Our knowledge and understanding, like the landscape around us, is constantly changing.

Opposite: Archaeologist Jakob Kainz with the 'Orkney Venus' figurine found at Links of Noltland in 2009.

Top: Two bone pins found at Links of Noltland.

Middle: A decorated slab and a pillow stone unveiled during the Ness of Brodgar excavations.

Bottom: Image drawn from geophysical survey of the Brodgar area.

Aside from Maeshowe and the Heart of Neolithic Orkney, there are more than 30 other Historic Scotland properties in Orkney, a few of which are shown below.

BROCH OF GURNESS

Substantial remains of an Iron Age broch overlooking Eynhallow Sound, surrounded by its own village and approached via an imposing causeway.

↗ Near Evie on the north-east coast of Mainland

🕐 Open summer only

📞 **01856 751414**

🚗 Approx. **12 miles** from Maeshowe

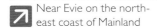

BROUGH OF BIRSAY

A Norse settlement, centred around a small Romanesque church, on a tidal island previously occupied by Picts.

↗ Near Birsay on the north-west coast of Mainland

🕐 Open mid-June to 30 Sept, when tides permit

📞 **01856 841815** (Skara Brae)

🚗 Approx. **14 miles** from Maeshowe

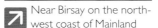

THE BISHOP'S AND EARL'S PALACE

The spectacular ruins of the Bishop of Orkney's medieval residence, enlarged around 1605 by Earl Patrick Stewart into a grandiose Renaissance complex.

↗ In the centre of Kirkwall

🕐 Open summer only

📞 **01856 871918**

🚗 Approx. **10 miles** from Maeshowe

HACKNESS BATTERY AND MARTELLO TOWER

Built to defend shipping during the Napoleonic Wars, these two distinctive installations offer a fascinating glimpse into life at a 19th-century military outpost.

↗ In South Walls, at the south-east tip of Hoy

🕐 Open summer only

📞 **01856 701727**

🚗 Approx. **25 miles** from Maeshowe

For information on all Historic Scotland properties, please visit our website: **www.historicenvironment.scot/visit-a-place**

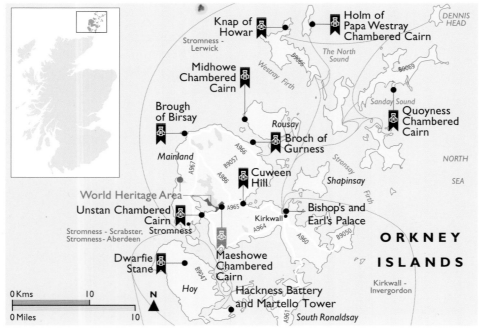

Car parking	P
Bus parking	P
Reasonable wheelchair access	
Interpretive display	
Shop	
Tea/coffee facilities	
Accessible by public transport	
Visitor centre	i
Restaurant/café	
Picnic area	
Disabled toilet	
Toilets	
Guided tours	
Dogs not permitted	
Children's quiz	